Hey Kids! Let's Visit Seattle

Fun, Facts, and Amazing Discoveries for Kids

Teresa Mills

Life Experiences Publishing

Copyright © 2023 by Teresa Mills

All rights reserved.

No portion of this book may be reproduced in any form without written permission from the publisher or author, except as permitted by U.S. copyright law.

Contents

Welcome	1
A Little About Seattle	3
1. Seattle Center	11
2. Seattle Waterfront	15
3. Pike Place Market	21
4. Seattle Aquarium	25
5. Seattle Great Wheel	33
6. Washington State Ferries	35
7. Seattle Center Monorail	37
8. Space Needle	41
9. Artists at Play Playground	45
10. Seattle Children's Museum	49
11. Pacific Science Center (PacSci)	53
12. Museum of Pop Culture (MoPop)	57
13. Chihuly Garden and Glass	61

14.	Bill and Melinda Gates Foundation Discovery Center	65
15.	The Columbia Center and Sky View Observatory	67
16.	Woodland Park Zoo	71
17.	The Museum of Flight	79
18.	Ballard (Hiram M. Chittenden) Locks	81
19.	Mount Rainier National Park	85
20.	Olympic National Park	89
21.	Seattle Underground Tours	95
22.	Whale Watching	99

Welcome

Seattle is located in the state of Washington, which is in the Pacific Northwest portion of the United States. Seattle is an awesome place to visit! It is full of many things to do and see including a zoo, a beautiful waterfront, a cool public market, and the Space Needle. Seattle's nickname is the Emerald City because it is filled with lush greenery all year long.

This book is written as a fun fact guide about some attractions and sites in Seattle. It includes some history interspersed with fun facts about things to do. The book can easily be enjoyed by younger children through reading it with them. You can visit Seattle right from your own home! Whether you are preparing for a vacation with the family or just want to learn a little more about the Emerald City, this book is for you.

As you continue to learn more about Seattle, I have some fun activity and coloring pages that you can download and print at:

https://kid-friendly-family-vacations.com/seattlefun

When you have completed this book, I invite you to enjoy the other books in the series. We visit Washington DC, a Cruise Ship, New York City, London England, San Francisco, Savannah Georgia, Paris France, Charleston South Carolina, Chicago, Boston, Rome Italy, Philadelphia, San Diego, Seoul South Korea, Atlanta, and Dublin Ireland!

Enjoy!

Teresa Mills

A Little About Seattle

Seattle is located in the Pacific Northwest portion of the United States in the state of Washington about 100 miles south of the border with Canada. The city of Seattle is on an isthmus (a narrow piece of land with water on both sides linking two larger areas of land) between Puget Sound and Lake Washington. The two maps in this chapter might help this make more sense.

Puget Sound is a body of water that is actually part of the Salish Sea (a small part of the Pacific Ocean around British Columbia, Canada, and Washington State). It also connects the Seattle area with the Pacific Ocean. Puget Sound is the body of water to the left (west) of Seattle on the map. A sound is an inlet of the ocean that is larger than a bay and usually has large open spaces of water.

Location of Seattle on a map

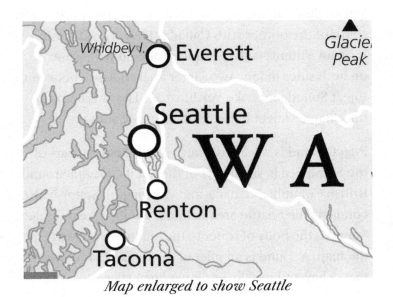
Map enlarged to show Seattle

The city of Seattle is named for the Duwamish Indian Leader Sealth (Si'ahl) who was very welcoming to the settlers of the area in 1851. The name became official when the first plats of for the town were filed on May 23, 1853.

Today, Seattle is a large metropolitan area. It is the most populated city in the Pacific Northwest and the state of Washington. It is also (at this time) the 15th largest metropolitan area in the United States and one of the largest ports in North America. Some large companies started business in Seattle including Red Robin, Starbucks, Boeing, Cinnabon, and Costco. The nearby city of Redmond is the home of Microsoft and Nintendo.

If you are into sports, Seattle has several major league teams:

- Seattle Seahawks (NFL – Football)
- Seattle Sounders FC (MLS – Soccer)
- Seattle Mariners (MLB – Baseball)
- Seattle Kraken (NHL – Ice Hockey)
- Seattle Storm (WNBA – Women's Basketball)
- Seattle Seawolves (MLR – Rugby)
- OL Reign (NWSL – Women's Soccer)

In this book, we will explore some of the most popular tourist attractions and learn a little history of Seattle along the way. We will even take a look at the city beneath the city that is the Seattle Underground!

So, are you ready?

Let's Visit Seattle!

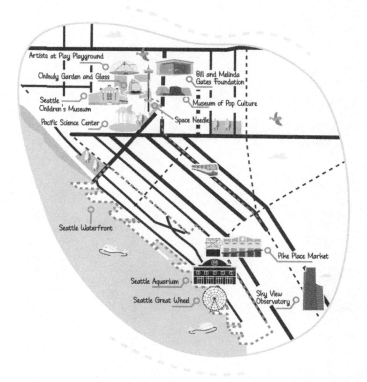

Map of Seattle Attractions

Map of Greater Seattle Area Attractions

Chapter 1
Seattle Center

The Seattle Center is an educational, arts, and tourism center that spans 74 acres (30 hectares). Many of the current features of the center were added for the 1962 World's Fair. The landmark feature of the center is the Space Needle. The Space Needle is 605 feet (184 meters) tall.

Seattle Center has been around in one form or another since 1927 when the Civic Auditorium and the Civic Arena were built. The land for these buildings came from land that was owned and donated by David and Louise Boren Denny who stipulated "public use forever" for the land. Money for the civic center came from James Osborne and was matched by public funding.

A big boom in construction came after the Center was chosen as the site of the 1962 World's Fair. A World's Fair theme of Space Exploration influenced many of the next structures that were built including the Space Needle, the monorail, and the International Fountain.

Seattle Center with the Seattle Skyline and Mt. Rainer in the background

Some of the things you can see at Seattle Center:

- Space Needle
- International Fountain
- Seattle Center Monorail
- John T. Williams Totem Pole
- Kobe Bell
- Artists at Play Playground
- Museum of Pop Culture (MoPop)
- Chihuly Garden and Glass
- Pacific Science Center

- Seattle Children's Museum
- Seattle Children's Theater

Many of these attractions are featured later in this book.

Fun Facts About Seattle Center

- Elvis Presley was onsite at the Seattle Center in 1962 to shoot the film *It Happened at the World's Fair.*

- After the World's Fair, one of the names suggested for the Seattle Center was Needleland (for the Space Needle).

- The City of Seattle purchased the monorail system from Century 21 (sponsors of the World's Fair) for $600,000.

Chapter 2
Seattle Waterfront

The Seattle Waterfront is a fun area of piers full of shops, attractions, and restaurants. There you will find the Seattle Aquarium and the Seattle Great Wheel. The Pike Place Market is a short walk up Pike Place Street.

Seattle Waterfront

Pier 50–52 is home to the different ferry services offered.

Along Pier 54, you will find Ivar's Acres of Clams restaurant and a few local businesses.

Ivar's Acres of Clams on Pier 54

Pier 55 houses some shops and a Starbucks Coffee Shop as well as the Burgandy Viscosi Art Gallery (a local Seattle artist).

HEY KIDS! LET'S VISIT SEATTLE

Pier 56 is home to a sailing service, Elliot's Oyster House, Wing Dome, and the engineering firm Mithun. The Mithun firm renovated the dock in 2000.

Elliott's Oyster House on Pier 56

Pier 57 is loaded with things to do and see. There you will find a carousel, a game room, stores, and places to grab some food. You will also see the Seattle Great Wheel on this pier.

Seattle Great Wheel on Pier 57

Pier 59-60 is home to the Seattle Aquarium.

Seattle Aquarium on Pier 59

Pier 62 is the place for cultural events as it is the home of the Seattle Waterfront Park. There are local food sellers, street art, and shows.

Pier 66 is the Bell Harbor and Bell Street Pier. Here you will find a convention center and fun places to eat. Pier 66 is also a cruise ship port for Norwegian Cruise Lines and Oceania Lines.

Pier 67 is home to the Brim Coffee House, the Edgewater Hotel, and the Six Seven Restaurant.

Pier 69 is where you will hop aboard the Victorian Clipper for sailings to Victoria, British Columbia, Canada, or for a whale watching excursion.

Pier 70 is an international trade storage facility.

Fun Facts About the Seattle Waterfront

- Occasionally it is possible to see the Aurora Borealis (the Northern Lights) from the Seattle Waterfront. The lights would be dim from town, but it is possible.

- The gold rush to the Klondike River in Canada put the Seattle Waterfront on the map as the "Gateway to Alaska."

- The Beatles stayed in the Edgewater Hotel on Pier 67 in 1964 during the height of Beatlemania in the US.

Chapter 3
Pike Place Market

Pike Place Market is a public market in downtown Seattle that has been open since August 17, 1907. The marketplace has more than 100 shops. Many people of Seattle consider the market to be "the soul of Seattle." Pike Place is one of the Seattle icons that locals actually want to visit and do visit! It's so popular that the market sees over 10 million visitors per year.

Pike Place Market was started in 1907 by 8 local farmers who wanted to sell produce direct to the public. Soon the market expanded to 76 stalls. By 1922, it had expanded to 11 buildings taking up 9 acres (3.64 hectares) close to the Seattle waterfront. However, the market never fully recovered from the effects of Executive Order 9066 during World War II, which forced almost 2/3 of the vendors, all of whom were of Japanese descent, into internment camps. The market was later saved by a historic district being built around the market. Today, the market has over 500 shops, restaurants, and vendors. Things that you will see at the Pike Place Market include flowers, fruits and veggies, fresh fish, cookies, candles, t-shirts, and many restaurants.

The Pike Place Market

HEY KIDS! LET'S VISIT SEATTLE 23

Fruit in the Pike Place Market

At Pike Place Market, there is a fish market called Pike Place Fish Market. When a customer purchases fish or some other seafood at the market, the fishmongers (a store or person who sells fish) will throw the fish to the cashier. The fishmonger yells the order, and the other fishmongers repeat it back in unison. This fish throwing tradition dates to 1980 when the owner of the fish market threw the first seafood.

Pike Place Fish Market

Fun Facts About The Pike Place Market

- The iconic neon sign "Public Market Center" and clock were installed at the market in 1937.

- The Three Girls Bakery opened at the market in 1912. It was the first Seattle business operated solely by women.

- There are close to 85 local farmers selling produce at the market.

Chapter 4

Seattle Aquarium

Aquariums are fun places to visit to see fish and other sea animals in their environments, but did you know that aquariums are also places where scientists and conservationists (people who work to protect and preserve the environment and wildlife) work? The scientists and conservationists at the aquarium spend their time learning more about the animals and their environments. The scientists in Seattle are learning about the sea animals in Puget Sound.

The Seattle Aquarium opened on May 20, 1977, and it is a part of Seattle's Waterfront. The aquarium is built right on Pier 59 and extends into Elliott Bay, which is part of Puget Sound right in downtown Seattle.

The Seattle Aquarium

HEY KIDS! LET'S VISIT SEATTLE

The animals housed in the Seattle Aquarium are a part of six major exhibits:

Windows on Washington Waters

This is a 120,000-gallon (450,000-liter) exhibit that is right at the front doors of the aquarium. The exhibit mimics the coastal waters of Washington. The exhibit has dive shows throughout the day. In this exhibit you might see rockfish, salmon, wolf eel, and sea anemones.

A diver with a wolf eel

Life on the Edge

This exhibit teaches about the sea life in Puget Sound tide pools. This is a hands-on exhibit that allows you to get up close and personal with the animals there. In this exhibit you may see hermit crabs, sea anemones, and sea stars.

Sea anemone

Pacific Coral Reef

This is a 25,000-gallon (95,000-liter) man-made coral reef exhibit. The fish that live in and around reefs that you might see here are the triggerfish, the pufferfish, and porcupinefish.

A triggerfish

Birds & Shores

This is an open-air exhibit that allows you to take a stroll through the rocky shorelines of Puget Sound. You will see many of the birds that make their life there including the common murre, the tufted puffin, the long-billed curlew, the black oystercatcher, and the rhinoceros auklet.

A tufted puffin

Underwater Dome

The largest habitat in the aquarium offers a 360-degree view into a 400,000-gallon (1,500,000-liter) environment. You will be able to see many Puget Sound fish here including the dogfish (a small shark that lives on the sea bottom) and the rockfish (a fish that can live up to 100 years).

A dogfish

Marine Mammals

River otters, sea otters, fur seals, and harbor seals can be found in the Marine Mammals exhibit.

A harbor seal

Fun Facts About The Seattle Aquarium

- The Seattle Aquarium is the 9th largest aquarium in the United States at this time.

- There is a fictional Seattle Aquarium featured in the action-adventure game *The Last of Us Part II*.

- The Seattle Aquarium is co-founder of a program called ReShark. ReShark is an international coalition in conservatism helping to recover the zebra shark in Indonesia.

Chapter 5

Seattle Great Wheel

The Seattle Great Wheel is a Ferris wheel that stands 175 feet (53.5 meters) tall. It's located at Pier 57 of the Seattle Waterfront. Each of the 42 gondolas can hold 8 passengers, and they provide unique views of the Seattle Waterfront. There is even a special reserved gondola with glass floors! The super special reserved gondola holds 4 passengers.

The wheel opened for passengers on June 29, 2012. At that time, Seattle was the third city in North America to have this type of wheel. The other two at that time were the Myrtle Beach SkyWheel and the Niagara SkyWheel.

The Seattle Giant Wheel

Fun Facts About the Seattle Great Wheel

- The Seattle Great Wheel has more than 500,000 LED lights. There are colorful light shows from the wheel every Friday, Saturday, and Sunday nights at 10 PM.

- When the Great Wheel opened in 2012, it was the tallest Ferris wheel on the United States' west coast.

- The Seattle Great Wheel has been featured in the 2017 film *Death Note* and is a landmark in the 2020 game *The Last of Us Part II*.

Chapter 6

Washington State Ferries

The Washington State Ferries are a part of the Washington State Department of Transportation. The Puget Sound routes of the Washington State Ferries are considered to be a part of the state highway system. This ferry system is the largest operated in the United States with more than 20 million people riding the ferries per year. This number goes up every year, so it is likely even more than that.

The ferry system operates a fleet of 21 along 10 different routes. The ferries carry passengers, bikes, and motor vehicles. The ferries are used by commuters to get to and from work across the Puget Sound as well as by tourists and truckers.

Two of the Washington State Ferries

Fun Facts About the Washington State Ferries

- The largest ferry in the Washington State Ferries system is the Jumbo Mark II class ferry. Each of these large ferries can carry up to 202 vehicles and 2,500 passengers.

- The main means of transportation on Puget Sound between the 1880s and the 1920s was a fleet of steam ships called the "mosquito fleet." This fleet was the beginnings of the Washington State Ferry system.

- The ferry system allows people to live just about anywhere along the shorelines and islands of Puget Sound but still be very much connected to the cities around them.

Chapter 7
Seattle Center Monorail

The Seattle Center Monorail was built to be used at the 1962 World's Fair. The construction was completed by Alweg Rapid Transit Systems, a German firm. Alweg offered to finance the $3.5 million (original estimate) cost of installing their system at no cost to the city or Century 21 (the fair organizers). To help get the $3.5 million investment back, Alweg would collect monorail fares, a surcharge on fair tickets, and concession revenues at the monorail terminals during the fair. If their investment was recouped during the World's Fair, Alweg would then turn over the system to Century 21. A contract was signed on December 22, 1960, with a revised construction cost of $4.2 million (to allow larger trains and stations), and construction began on April 6, 1961, with a groundbreaking ceremony.

The monorail system opened to the public on March 24, 1962. This was one month before the start of the 1962 World's Fair. During the 6 months of the World's Fair, the monorail carried more that 8 million guests. The construction cost was easily recovered by Alweg Rapid Transit Systems, and the monorail system was turned over to Century 21. In April of 1965. Century 21 sold the monorail system to the city of Seattle for $600,000.

The Seattle Center Monorail

The system has two trains that travel the route between the Westlake Monorail Station and Seattle Center every 10 minutes. The system operates up to 16 hours per day. In addition to being a major tourist attraction, the monorail system is a part of the public transportation system of Seattle.

HEY KIDS! LET'S VISIT SEATTLE

Fun Facts About the Seattle Center Monorail

- The trip between the Westlake Center and the Seattle Center takes about 2 minutes.

- The monorail was featured in the 1963 musical *It Happened at the World's Fair*. This film starred Elvis Presley and was filmed during the 1962 World's Fair. The monorail has also been featured in *Love Happens, Frasier, The Man in the High Castle, Assassins,* and *Grassroots*.

- The two trains that are a part of the monorail system are the original trains from 1962.

Chapter 8
Space Needle

The Space Needle, which opened on April 21, 1962, is located in the Seattle Center. It was built for the 1962 World's Fair and is considered to be an icon of the city of Seattle. It is 605 feet (184 meters) tall and is built to withstand winds of 200 miles/hour (320 km/hour). It can also withstand an earthquake of 9.0 magnitude.

The "flying saucer" shaped top and the hourglass shaped tower designs were a compromise between two architects, John Graham Jr. and Victor Steinbrueck. Construction took 8 months and was completed in December 1961. The theme of the 1962 World's Fair was space, so the paint used on the needle was named for that theme – "Astronaut White" for the legs, "Orbital Olive" for the core of the structure, "Re-entry Red" for the halo, and "Galaxy Gold" for the sunburst and pagoda roof.

The Space Needle

HEY KIDS! LET'S VISIT SEATTLE

Fun Facts about the Space Needle

- On April Fools' Day (April 1) of 1989, the Almost Live comedy show of KING-TV ran a spoofed news bulletin. The bulletin announced that the Space Needle had fallen. They even had a mocked-up graphic of the tower ruins on the ground. The prank overwhelmed the Seattle 911 system.

- The Space Needle is shown on the introductions of many TV shows and movies to explain that the show is set in Seattle. Some of these shows are *Frasier, Grey's Anatomy,* and *Bill Nye the Science Guy*.

- Six people with parachutes have jumped from the tower since it opened. Four were part of a legal (pre-authorized) jump in 1996. The other two jumps were illegal, and the jumpers were arrested.

Chapter 9

Artists at Play Playground

Artists at Play is a playground at the Seattle Center. The playground can be seen from the top of the Space Needle and is close to the Museum of Pop Culture (MoPop).

The playground was developed by two artists, Trimpin and Judith Caldwell, who were eager to create a space to encourage creative play. It is located on a piece of land that contained the World's Fair Fun Forest rides and amusements until they were taken apart and removed in 2011. For four years, there was only an empty concrete slab where the playground is now. The playground opened in 2015.

Artists at Play playground as seen from the Space Needle

The playground combines art and creativity. This can be seen from some of the structures around the park:

- There is a labyrinth in the playground. A labyrinth is a little like a maze, but with one entrance that follows a circular path to the center of the design. In some cultures, a labyrinth is used for meditative (relaxing) walking.

- There is a rebus (a puzzle that combines pictures and letters to form the answer) at the center of the labyrinth.

- There is a letter tree with the letters connected by cranks, each corresponding to a musical note.

HEY KIDS! LET'S VISIT SEATTLE

- There are giant earphones at listening stations.

- The Pebble Play Station allows kids to place handfuls of pebbles down stump sculptures, resulting in musical sounds.

- The Rain Stick helps kids learn cause and effect.

- The Song Fence can be played like a giant pan flute.

- Sound Swings send vibrations to artwork above the swings.

- Bronze Poems is a section that shows rhyming verses describing the animal kingdom.

- Story Lines are picture imaginations by children bringing together sound, motion, and adventure.

Fun Facts about the Artists at Play playground

- Local kids had input into the design of the playground. The playground project team met with kids at open houses, presentations, and workshops to get ideas for what to include in the playground. The children were invited to submit drawings of what they would like the playground to look like.

- To bring nature into the play place, real boulders and rocks with indentions were added. There are also natural logs with peeling bark and bugs.

- There is a child-sized sky walk in the playground with an ADA-friendly (American's with Disabilities Act) cabin, slide, and dish-shaped swings.

Chapter 10
Seattle Children's Museum

The Seattle Children's Museum is located on the ground floor of the Foundry Building (housing a large food court) at the Seattle Center. The museum was founded in 1979 and currently has 11 exhibits in over 18,000 square feet (1,672 square meters) of play space. This might be a better museum for younger kids in your family, but there are some fun things to explore there.

Seattle Children's Museum entrance

The museum caters to children ages 6 months to 8 years old with interactive play exhibits such as:

The Neighborhood – play in a local supermarket, a place to care for animals, and deliver packages door to door.

Tribal Tales – learn from local Coast Salish tribes through storytelling and puppets.

Mountain – track wildlife and explore the plants of the Pacific Northwest.

Corner Workshop – a place to tinker and create.

Raindrop Reading Room – cozy up with some good books.

HEY KIDS! LET'S VISIT SEATTLE 51

Play area in the Children's Museum from the floor above

Fun Facts about the Seattle Children's Museum

- The museum has some rotating activities that include nature encounters, story times, science workshops, and creative art.

- In the mountain (pictured above), you can follow a winding path, crawl inside a log, hide in a marmot's den, and stand under a waterfall.

- There is an imagination Studio Art Area with paint and clay provided.

Chapter 11
Pacific Science Center (PacSci)

The Pacific Science Center (PacSci) was founded as the United States' first science and technology center. Its main goal is to ignite curiosity in every child and fuel a passion for critical thinking, experimentation, and discovery in everyone. The science center was designed for the 1962 World's Fair.

The science center has 8 buildings including 2 IMAX theaters. It also has one of the largest Laser Dome theaters in the world. There are hundreds of science exhibits throughout the center.

Pacific Science Center

Attractions and Exhibits at the Pacific Science Center include:

IMAX Theater – There are two IMAX theaters at the science center, the PACCAR and the Boeing. The Boeing IMAX theater shows some of the latest movies in 2D and 3D. The PACCAR theater shows a variety of shorter documentary type films.

Laser Dome – This theater displays concerts on the large dome. The shows available vary from Led Zeppelin to Queen to Pink Floyd to Taylor Swift!

Planetarium – The planetarium offers live, immersive presentations exploring our universe or planets in our solar system.

HEY KIDS! LET'S VISIT SEATTLE

Exhibits – There are many ongoing exhibits as well as temporary exhibits that are changed out at different times. The permanent exhibits include a tropical butterfly house, a model of Puget Sound, Adventures with Sound, and the Saltwater Tide Pool.

Fun Facts about the Pacific Science Center

- The Boeing IMAX screen is 60 feet (18.3 meters) tall and 80 feet (24.4 meters) wide. The PACCAR screen is 37 feet (11.3 meters) tall and 60 feet (18.3 meters) wide.

- The architect who designed PacSci was Minoru Yamaski. Later, he was the architect of the World Trade Center in New York City.

- The Pacific Science Center has a school outreach program called Science on Wheels that provides hands-on science education.

Chapter 12

Museum of Pop Culture (MoPop)

The Museum of Pop Culture (MoPop) is located in the Seattle Center. It originally opened as the Experience Music Project (later just EMP) in 2000. The founder was Paul Allen, co-founder of Microsoft. The 140,000-square-foot (13,000-square-meter) metallic looking wonder was designed by architect Frank O. Gehry.

The museum went through several other name changes over the years. After being known as EMP for a while, it became Experience Music Project and Science Fiction Museum and Hall of Fame (EMPSFM), and then simply the EMP Museum. Then in November of 2016, the museum became known as the Museum of Pop Culture (MoPop).

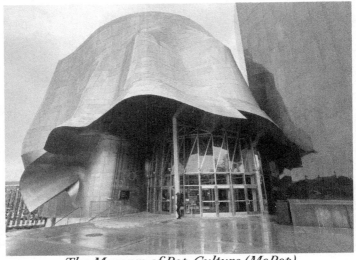

The Museum of Pop Culture (MoPop)

Inside MoPop you will see exhibits about pop culture of all types including science fiction, video games, fantasy, and horror. On display are costumes from the *Wizard of Oz, Harry Potter,* and *The Lord of the Rings*. You will see props and costumes from *Star Wars, Ghostbusters, Galaxy Quest,* and *Terminator*. Horror movie fans can explore props and costumes from *The Walking Dead, Friday the 13th,* and Michael Jackson's *Thriller* music video.

Music fans will love seeing the giant sculpture of 700 instruments in a tree that is on display and pays homage (tribute) to the guitar. The sculpture is called "IF VI WAS IX: Roots and Branches." The also museum houses one of the world's largest collections of handwritten lyrics, personal instruments and photographs, and artifacts of Jimi Hendrix (a Seattle-born musician) and the band Nirvana. Hands-on educational music exhibits like the Sound Lab and On Stage allow visitors to perform.

Fun Facts about the Museum of Pop Culture (MoPop)

- The exterior (outside) of the building looks a lot like a smashed electric guitar, a symbol of rock and rollers everywhere.

- The 40-foot (12.2-meter) tall video wall called "Sky Church" is a centerpiece of the museum. This is one of the largest indoor LED screens in the world. Music videos play through the very sophisticated sound system.

- In the "IF VI WAS IX: Roots and Branches" sculpture, there are 40 custom made, computer controlled self-playing guitars. The guitars play some of sculptor Gerhard Trimpin's music.

Chapter 13
Chihuly Garden and Glass

Chihuly Garden and Glass is an exhibit that displays and showcases the glass work of artist Dale Chihuly. The museum opened in May of 2012 in Seattle Center.

The Garden and Glass exhibition is made up of three sections: the Garden, the Glasshouse, and all of the Interior Exhibits. The centerpiece of the Glasshouse is a 100-foot (30.5-meter) glasswork display that is one of Chihuly's largest sculptures.

Chihuly Garden and Glass

Dale Chihuly is a native of Tacoma, Washington. He learned about glass during his studies at the University of Washington. He continued his studies at the University of Wisconsin at the first glass program in the United States. He then completed his studies at the Rhode Island School of Design (RISD). Chihuly then started a program at RISD and taught there for more than 10 years.

Chihuly's work is a part of more than 200 museum collections worldwide. He is the creator of many famous series of works including:

1970s – *Cylinders and Baskets*

1980s – *Seaforms, Macchia, Venetians*

HEY KIDS! LET'S VISIT SEATTLE

1990s – *Niijima Floats and Chandeliers*

2000s – *Fiori*

Chihuly has works displayed over the piazzas and canals of Venice in Italy, the Victoria and Albert Museum in London, Garfield Park Conservatory in Chicago, and this exhibit in Seattle.

Glass work outside Chihuly Garden and Glass

Fun Facts about Dale Chihuly

- His sculptures were incorporated into the Biltmore Estates Gardens (Asheville, NC) in 2018.

- The Bellagio in Las Vegas has a large sculpture on display by Chihuly in the lobby.

- Chihuly's first glass pieces were pieces woven into tapestries instead of glass blown into fancy chandeliers and creations.

Chapter 14

Bill and Melinda Gates Foundation Discovery Center

The Bill and Melinda Gates Foundation Discovery Center is across 5th Avenue from Seattle Center at 440 5th Ave N. The Discovery Center is a series of five galleries that lead you through an exploration of the history of the Bill and Melinda Gates Foundation. The museum explores the innovations and inventions that are helping to create a world where we all have an opportunity to lead healthy and productive lives.

Bill Gates, one of the founders of Microsoft Corporation, and his wife Melinda formed the Bill and Melinda Gates Foundation in 2000. The foundation grew from the combination of the William H. Gates Foundation that was formed in 1994 and the

Gates Learning Foundation, which created local and world-wide programs to benefit education and health. Bill and Melinda were able to transfer $20 billion in Microsoft stock to the foundation to get it started, and later William Buffet donated to the foundation.

Since 2000, the foundation has spent more than $50 billion to help make a difference in the world. This Discovery Center helps spread the word about some of those projects.

Fun Facts about Bill and Melinda Gates

- Bill Gates is most well-known as one of the co-founders of the Microsoft Corporation. He wrote his first computer program when he was 13 years old. The game he wrote allowed a player to play tic-tac-toe against the computer. The program was written in BASIC (a computer programming language) on a school computer.

- As of January 2021, Bill Gates was ranked as the third richest person in the world.

- Melinda began her career at Microsoft in 1987 after receiving her MBA (Master of Business Administration) at Duke University. She became the General Manager of Information Products at Microsoft before she and Bill were married in 1994.

Chapter 15
The Columbia Center and Sky View Observatory

The Sky View Observatory is an observatory on the rooftop of the Columbia Center in downtown Seattle. The Columbia Center is a 76-story (933-feet / 284-meter) tall building located at 701 5th Avenue. At the time of this writing, it is the tallest building in Seattle and in the entire state of Washington. The Columbia Center was previously named the Bank of America Tower and Columbia Seafirst Center.

The Sky View Observatory is located on the 73rd floor of the Columbia Center building. This view from 902 feet (275 meters) offers the highest view of Seattle and the surrounding area. You will take in a 360-degree panoramic view that includes:

- Mt. Rainier
- Bellevue, Washington
- The city of Seattle and the Space Needle
- The Olympic Mountains
- The Cascade Mountains
- Mt. Baker
- Elliott Bay

The Columbia Center and Skyview Observatory

Fun Facts about the Columbia Center and Sky View Observatory

- The first three floors of the Columbia Center house a huge food court.

- The Columbia Center, when it was completed in 1985, was not a welcome addition to Seattle. It fundamentally changed the downtown landscape, and that made some residents upset.

- Annually, the Columbia Center hosts the largest firefighter competition in the world. The local Leukemia and Lymphoma society is the beneficiary of this meeting of 1300 firefighters from around the world racing up 69 floors (1,311 steps) in full firefighting gear.

Chapter 16
Woodland Park Zoo

The Woodland Park Zoo is located about 10 minutes north of downtown Seattle at 5500 Phinney Ave. N. The zoo is a non-profit organization dedicated to saving wildlife. The zoo began as a small group of animals on the estate of Guy C. Phinney. Mr. Phinney was a real estate developer and a lumber mill owner. When Mr. Phinney died, his wife sold Woodland Park – a 188-acre (76-hectare) park to the city of Seattle for $5,000 and the agreement that they take over the $95,000 mortgage. At the time, the mayor thought that price was too high, but city council voted to buy the park anyway.

At the zoo, you can see these exhibits:

African Savanna

This area contains animals that are native to the African grasslands. Here you will see herbivores such as zebras, ostriches, and giraffes. There are also enclosures for small savanna birds, Patas monkeys, hippopotamus, and African lions.

A Hippopotamus

Assam Rhino Reserve

This area is home to two young Greater One-Horned rhinos. This is an exhibit that follows the zoo's mission to save wildlife. The zoo is working to protect and defend this type of rhino from illegal trade.

A Greater One-Horned Rhino

HEY KIDS! LET'S VISIT SEATTLE

Australia

Enjoy the animals of the wider Pacific Ocean area including New Zealand, Australia, New Guinea, and many islands of the South Pacific. Here you may see kookaburras, snow leopards, wallabies, and emu.

A Kookaburra

Molbak's Butterfly Garden

This is a garden full of butterflies. The exhibit teaches the butterfly's life cycle, and there is a space to see new butterflies emerging from their chrysalises.

Humboldt Penguin Exhibit

This area houses penguins from the arid, coastal regions of Peru. You will see Humboldt penguins living along a rocky coast. The waters are warmed and cooled geothermally (with heat energy from the earth).

Humboldt Penguins

Living Northwest Trail

Here you may see animals from the Northwest region of the United States and Canada such as the Canada lynx, brown bears, gray wolves, and river otters.

A Canada Lynx

HEY KIDS! LET'S VISIT SEATTLE

Temperate Forest

Temperate forests are the type found in the Pacific Northwest. This section of the zoo features animals such as the red panda, maned wolves, Asian cranes, and Chilean flamingos. This section of the zoo also has an animal contact area featuring goats and sheep.

Chilean Flamingos

Trail of Adaptations

This section of the zoo features a variety of animals showing off their unique features. In this area, you may see Indian flying foxes, meerkats, Egyptian tortoises, or Komodo dragons.

A Komodo Dragon

Tropical Asia

This section showcases some of the endangered species of the tropical forests of Asia. Here you may see animals such as sloth bears, orangutans, Malayan Tapirs, Malayan Tigers, siamangs, warty pigs, or langurs.

A Malayan Tiger

Tropical Rainforest

The tropical rainforest features many animals seen in rainforests. Some of the animals that you may see here are gorillas, lemurs, jaguars, toucans, tarantulas, saki monkeys, and colobus monkeys.

A Toucan

Lemurs

Fun Facts about the Woodland Park Zoo

- The Woodland Park Zoo was founded in 1899.

- The zoo was home to Bobo, a western lowland gorilla, from 1953 to 1968. Bobo was unique as he was raised in a family home. Bobo was very famous at the zoo and helped draw many visitors before the Seattle Center was built.

- A baby giraffe was born at the zoo in 2017. At birth, Lulu was 149 pounds (67.6 kg) and 5 feet 7 inches (1.7 meters) tall.

Chapter 17
The Museum of Flight

The Museum of Flight is located south of Seattle at 9404 East Marginal Way S. With more than 175 spacecraft and aircraft, the museum is the largest independent, non-profit air and space museum in the whole world. The museum also houses rare photos, exhibits and experiences, a library, and many artifacts.

The museum started in 1965 in a 10,000-square-foot (929-square-meter) space at the Seattle Center after the World's Fair. When the Red Barn (the birthplace of Boeing) was saved from being demolished and moved to its current location in 1983, this became the permanent home of the Museum of Flight.

One of the many aircraft on display at the Museum of Flight

Fun Facts about the Museum of Flight

- The museum has a Concorde 214 on display. This is one of four on display outside of Europe.

- The *City of Everett*, the first flight-worthy Boeing 747, is on display. This plane was named for the city of Everett, Washington and was retired in 1990.

- There is a restoration facility at the museum. There are always on-going restoration projects occurring here.

Chapter 18

Ballard (Hiram M. Chittenden) Locks

The Ballard Locks, also known as the Hiram M. Chittenden Locks, link Puget Sound with Lake Washington and Lake Union. The locks were completed in 1917. The locks are necessary as the waters of Lake Washington and Lake Union are 22 feet (6.7 meters) higher than the waters of Puget Sound at low tide.

But, you might ask, what is a lock and how does it work?

To be simple, you can think of a lock as an elevator for ships and boats. But why would we need an elevator for ships and boats?

In this case, there was discussion to create a connection between Lake Washington and Puget Sound since in 1854, there was no way to move from one to the other. A connection was needed to move logs, fishing boats, and milled lumber from one place to another easier.

The Ballard (Hiram M. Chittenden) Locks

Through many discussions and planning by the Army Corps of Engineers, the project to build a canal between Puget Sound and Lake Washington began initially in 1906 and then moved quicker 5 years later under the command of Hiram M. Chittenden. Because Puget Sound is saltwater and Lakes Union and Washington are fresh water and the lake levels differ from sea level, there were many engineering problems to overcome. The solution was to build the locks and a series of canals. The locks are the first part of this complex system that connects Puget Sound to Lake Union and then to Lake Washington.

The Ballard locks (to make things simple) have the following functions:

- To help keep the water level of Lake Washington

HEY KIDS! LET'S VISIT SEATTLE

and Lake Union at 20-22 feet (6.1-6.7 meters) above sea level.

- To prevent the mixing of saltwater and fresh water.

- To move boats from the level of the lake to the level of the sound.

Fun Facts about the Ballard Locks

- The locks offer another advantage: they have a fish ladder which helps with the migration of salmon to the sea. Salmon are anadromous (they hatch in river, lakes, and streams).

- The engineering project also lowered the lake levels of Lake Union and Lake Washington by 8.8 feet (2.7 meters) to make the system work properly. This created miles of new waterfront land.

- There are free walking tours of the locks from May-October.

Chapter 19

Mount Rainier National Park

The Mount Rainier National Park is close to 59 miles (95 km) south-southeast of Seattle. Mount Rainier is a part of the Cascade Mountain range in the Pacific Northwest. Its height is 14,417 feet (4,394 meters), making it the tallest mountain in the state of Washington.

Mount Rainier is spectacular and can be seen from downtown Seattle parks and observatories on clear days. Even though you can see it from the city, it is worth a trip to the National Park for an up-close and personal visit.

There are many hiking trails at the National Park. There are also hiking and climbing opportunities on the glaciers around Mount Rainier and on Mount Rainier itself.

Entrance to Mount Rainier National Park

Mount Rainier

HEY KIDS! LET'S VISIT SEATTLE

Fun Facts about Mount Rainier

- Mount Rainier is an active stratovolcano, also known as a composite volcano. A composite volcano is built up of many layers of hardened lava (molten or partially molten rock that leaks or erupts from a volcano) and tephra (fragmented material that comes from an eruption of a volcano).

- Mount Rainer is on the Decade Volcanoes list. This list contains 16 volcanoes that show more than one volcanic hazard, are located in populated areas, and show recent geological activities. The name Decade is because the list was started in the 1990s as part of the United Nations Decade for Natural Disaster Reduction.

- The most recent eruption activity recorded on Mount Rainier was between 1820 and 1854.

Chapter 20
Olympic National Park

Olympic National Park is located on the Olympic Peninsula, a large area of Washington State that lies west of Seattle across Puget Sound. Olympic National Park is very large, covering nearly 1,000,000 acres (404,685.6 hectares). It is vast and offers several distinctly different ecosystems to visit. There are old-growth temperate rainforests, glacier-capped mountains, and over 70 miles (112.6 km) of wild coastline.

Entrance to the Hoh Rainforest in Olympic National Park

Coastline

The coastline portion of Olympic stretches along the Pacific coast of Washington for more than 70 miles (112.6 km). The beach has many unbroken stretches of wilderness that are 10-20 miles (16-32 km) long each. Some of the beaches are rocky and some are sandy. There are some opportunities for hiking.

HEY KIDS! LET'S VISIT SEATTLE

Ruby Beach along the Olympic National Park coastline

Glacier-capped Mountains

The center of the National Park contains the Olympic Mountains. The sides and ridgelines of the mountains are topped with massive glaciers. Olympic National Park offers hiking and mountain climbing.

Olympic Mountains

Rainforests

The Hoh and Quinault rainforests are located in the western portion of the national park. The rainforests get over 12 feet (3.70 meters) or rain per year. These rainforests are temperate rainforests that are dominated by coniferous trees (cone bearing trees). There are many hiking trails throughout this section of the park.

Hoh Rainforest in Olympic National Park

Fun Facts about Olympic National Park

- There are over 3,000 miles (4,828 km) of rivers and streams in the National Park.

- There are over 600 miles (965 km) of trails in the park.

- The Olympic Mountain glaciers make up a huge part of the most glacier covered area of the lower 48 of the United States.

Chapter 21
Seattle Underground Tours

Pioneer Square is Seattle's oldest neighborhood – the birthplace of Seattle. It is located in the southwest corner of downtown, just down from the ferry station on the waterfront. Pioneer Square was once the heart of the city as settlers arrived there in 1852.

Most of the buildings in Pioneer Square were wooden. Most of the wooden buildings were destroyed in the Great Seattle Fire on June 6, 1889. After the fire, the city required buildings be masonry (stonework). To help maintain the sewer system and basically get the city off of flood prone, muddy land, the roads were re-graded and built one to two stories higher.

Pioneer Square Today

The street re-grading project added concrete retaining walls on both sides of the old streets, filled in the space with dirt, and paved new roads overtop – raising the streets. Even though this was going on, the shop owners were eager to get back to business. They built new buildings on the old, muddy streets not really thinking that the storefronts they were building were eventually going to become basements. As time passed, sidewalk construction bridged the gap between the new roads and the second stories of the new buildings, creating the Seattle underground.

As time marched on and Seattle grew, many businesses moved uptown, and the Pioneer Square area fell into disrepair. Pioneer Square lay unused for quite a few years. A local publicist by the name of Bill Speidel started to research the area around Pioneer Square and started mentioning things to the local newspaper about the square and the ruins of an early Seattle. Speidel did eventually find the early city and was asked in May of 1965 (during the 'Know Your Seattle Day' by the Junior Chamber of Commerce) to give tours for $1 of the underground city. Speidel and his wife did give tours that day – 500 of them.

Bill Speidel started his official tour of the Underground after that. He also diligently collected signatures on a petition asking the city to designate Pioneer Square as a Historic Site. Bill's underground tour still operates today. Here are underground tour options:

Bill Speidel's Seattle Underground Tour

This tour is a 75-minute guided walking tour. The tour guides include a ton of information and a lot of entertainment into this short time. The tour starts in a theater under Doc Maynard's Public House with a little history of several early Seattle personalities. The tour continues through Pioneer Square with a little more history. Then the tour descends down into the Seattle Underground with some more history. You will see old Seattle buildings and learn how the roads were paved to create what is now the underground area.

Beneath the Streets Underground History Tours

Beneath the Streets has been providing public tours of the Seattle underground since 2013. This tour uses different areas of the underground network than the Bill Speidel tour. Beneath the Streets shows three of the underground areas. Their mission is to provide historically accurate guided tours that embrace the imperfect, illustrious, and fascinating truths of early Seattle.

Fun Facts about the Seattle Underground

- The original city of Seattle was very dangerous and subject to massive flooding as it was barely above sea level.

- The new streets (after the fire in 1889) were designed to be 12 feet (3.66 meters) higher than the original streets.

- As the new roads were being constructed (which took a few years to complete), walkways were at the new ground level, but shop entrances were 12 feet (3.66 meters) below. You would have to climb down a ladder to enter a business for a while.

Chapter 22
Whale Watching

Whale spotting can be exciting – the animals are magnificent! Whale watching is seasonal, so it is not available year-round. Most whale watching excursions are available April-December.

A Humpback Whale

Here are some companies that offer whale watching in the Seattle area.

Puget Sound Express

Puget Sound Express, a member of the Pacific Whale Watch Association, hosts whale watching tours from Edmonds, Washington. Edmonds is about 20 miles (32.2 km) from downtown Seattle. They offer 4- to 5-hour whale watching cruises late April through December.

Seattle Orca Whale Watching

This company offers whale watching cruises from Friday Harbor in the San Juan Islands March – October. The San Juan Islands are approximately 100 miles (161 km) from Seattle and require a ferry ride. They offer a classic tour that is best for young children and older adults as well as an adventure whale watching cruise for ages 8 and older.

FRS Clipper

The FRS Clipper offers 3- to 5-hour whale watching tours from downtown Seattle. This tour leaves from Pier 69 on the Seattle Waterfront. The tours are given May-October.

I hope you enjoyed your trip to Seattle! I have a fun puzzle and coloring page download to go along with the book. This fun addition is free to download here:

https://kid-friendly-family-vacations.com/seattlefun

Please consider adding a review to help other readers learn more about Seattle whether traveling or learning from home. Thanks!

kid-friendly-family-vacations.com/review-seattle

Also By Teresa Mills and Kid Friendly Family Vacations

Hey Kids! Let's Visit Washington DC
Hey Kids! Let's Visit A Cruise Ship
Hey Kids! Let's Visit New York City
Hey Kids! Let's Visit London England
Hey Kids! Let's Visit San Francisco
Hey Kids! Let's Visit Savannah Georgia
Hey Kids! Let's Visit Paris France
Hey Kids! Let's Visit Charleston South Carolina
Hey Kids! Let's Visit Chicago
Hey Kids! Let's Visit Rome Italy
Hey Kids! Let's Visit Boston
Hey Kids! Let's Visit Philadelphia
Hey Kids! Let's Visit San Diego
Hey Kids! Let's Visit Seattle
Hey Kids! Let's Visit Seoul South Korea
Hey Kids! Let's Visit Atlanta
Hey Kids! Let's Visit Dublin Ireland

More from Kid Friendly Family Vacations

BOOKS

Books to help build your kids / grandkids life experiences through travel and learning
https://kid-friendly-family-vacations.com/books

COLORING AND ACTIVITY PAGKAGES

Coloring pages, activity books, printable travel journals, and more in our Etsy shop
https://kid-friendly-family-vacations.com/etsy

RESOURCES FOR TEACHERS

Resources for teachers on Teachers Pay Teachers
https://kid-friendly-family-vacations.com/tpt

It is our mission to help you build your children's and grand-children's life experiences through travel. Not just traveling with your kids... building their Life Experiences"! Join our community here:
https://kid-friendly-family-vacations.com/join

Acknowledgements

Cover Photos

Seattle Great Wheel - © cestes001 / depositphotos.com

Pike Place Market – sign - © bildradar / depositphotos.com

Space Needle - © wirestock_creators / depositphotos.com

Woodland Park Zoo - humboldt penguin - © slowmotoingli / depositphotos.com

Mt. Rainier National Park - © Kid Friendly Family Vacations

Photos in Book

Map of Seattle - ©Furian / depositphotos.com

Seattle Waterfront - © CascadeCreatives / depositphotos.com

Seattle Waterfront – Ivars – © Kid Friendly Family Vacations

Seattle Waterfront – Elliotts – © Kid Friendly Family Vacations

Seattle Great Wheel - © cestes001 / depositphotos.com

Seattle Aquarium - © Kid Friendly Family Vacations

Pike Place Market – sign - © bildradar / depositphotos.com

Pike Place Market – veggies - © neelsky / depositphotos.com

Pike Place Fish Market - © Kid Friendly Family Vacations

Seattle Aquarium - wolf eel - © thediver123 / depositphotos.com

Seattle Aquarium - sea anemone - © kelpfish / depositphotos.com

Seattle Aquarium – triggerfish - © Aristrobd / depositphotos.com

Seattle Aquarium - tufted puffin - © Tarpan / depositphotos.com

Seattle Aquarium – dogfish - © thediver123 / depositphotos.com

Seattle Aquarium - harbor seal - © DesignPicsInc / depositphotos.com

HEY KIDS! LET'S VISIT SEATTLE

Washington State Ferries - © billperry / depositphotos.com

Seattle Center - © Rigucci / depositphotos.com

Seattle Center - monorail - © Kid Friendly Family Vacations

Space Needle - © wirestock_creators / depositphotos.com

Artists at Play Playground - © Kid Friendly Family Vacations

Seattle Children's Museum – entrance - © Kid Friendly Family Vacations

Seattle Children's Museum - © Kid Friendly Family Vacations

Pacific Science Center - © Kid Friendly Family Vacations

Museum of Pop Culture (MoPop) - © Kid Friendly Family Vacations

Chihuly Garden and Glass - © Kid Friendly Family Vacations

Chihuly Garden and Glass – sculpture - © Kid Friendly Family Vacations

Skyview Observatory - Columbia Center - © nadik29 / depositphotos.com

Woodland Park Zoo – hippo - © YAY_images / depositphotos.com

Woodland Park Zoo – rhino - © imagex / depositphotos.com

Woodland Park Zoo – kookaburra - © izanbar / depositphotos.com

Woodland Park Zoo - humboldt penguin - © slowmotoingli / depositphotos.com

Woodland Park Zoo - canada lynx- © natmacstock / depositphotos.com

Woodland Park Zoo - Chilean flamingos - © FOTO4440 / depositphotos.com

Woodland Park Zoo - komodo dragon - © SURZet / depositphotos.com

Woodland Park Zoo - malayan tiger - © wrangel / depositphotos.com

Woodland Park Zoo – toucan - © gmc3101 / depositphotos.com

Woodland Park Zoo - lemurs - © gmc3101 / depositphotos.com

Museum of Flight - © kip02kas / depositphotos.com

Hiram M. Chittenden (Ballard) Locks - © dbvirago / depositphotos.com

HEY KIDS! LET'S VISIT SEATTLE

Mt. Rainier National Park - © Kid Friendly Family Vacations

Olympic National Park – sign - © Kid Friendly Family Vacations

Olympic National Park - Ruby Beach - © zrfphoto / depositphotos.com

Olympic National Park - glacier topped mountains - © appalachianview / depositphotos.com

Seattle Underground – Pioneer Square - © iriana88w / depositphotos.com

Whale watching – humpback whale - © GUDKOVANDREY / depositphotos.com

About the Author

Teresa Mills is the bestselling author of the "Hey Kids! Let's Visit..." Book Series for Kids! Teresa's goal through her books and website is to help parents / grandparents who want to build the life experiences of their children / grandchildren through travel and learning activities.

She is an active mother and Mimi. She and her family love traveling in the USA, and internationally too! They love exploring new places, eating cool foods, and having yet another adventure as a family! With the Mills, it's all about traveling as family.

In addition to traveling, Teresa enjoys reading, hiking, biking, and helping others.

Join in the fun at

kid-friendly-family-vacations.com

Made in the USA
Monee, IL
06 July 2024